CELLO
Prep
Test

Rivers Centre.
Humber Way
Bletchley.
MK3 7PH.

This book belongs to: Scarlett John.

Date of Prep Test: Weds 27th March
2·42 pm.

Examiner's signature:

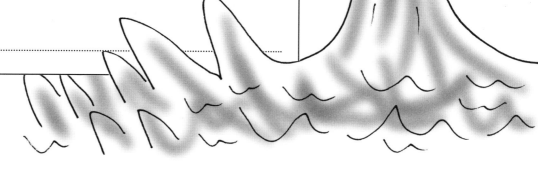

ABRSM

CELLO PREP TEST

Dear cello player,

Welcome to your Prep Test book – you are now on your way to receiving your first cello certificate! Though the Prep Test is not an exam, you will be playing to an ABRSM examiner, who will write comments and suggestions on your certificate, ready to give you at the end. Two particular skills your examiner will be listening out for as you go through the Tunes, Pieces and Listening Games, are playing right notes and keeping well in time – with a firm, steady pulse. These are both very important elements of music making, and will be the foundations of your future musical success.

The Prep Test is designed to be an enjoyable experience, and I hope you will feel pleased and proud to take your certificate away with you on the day. It will always be a reminder of your hard work and achievement during this early stage of your musical learning journey.

I very much hope too that you will enjoy showing the examiner what you can do, and that your Prep Test will be the start of a long voyage of exciting musical discovery and fun.

Good luck!

John Holmes
Chief Examiner

AB 3420

1 Tunes

The examiner will want to hear you play all three of these tunes. You will have to play them from memory, so once you have learnt them remember to keep your book closed when you are practising!

a) Walking in the Park

A straight bow and clean, precise strokes will help to make this tune really sing. Make sure to drop your elbow for the notes near the end.

b) Slimy Spaghetti

Try getting your left-hand fingers to curl. Remember to listen out for smooth bow changes.

Smoothly gliding ♩= c.72

mf

c) The School Run

Keep your left hand in time with the bow to avoid tripping up. Off you go!

Energetic, but steady ♩= c.76

f

2 Set Piece

Your set piece can be either one of the three pieces printed on pages 6, 7 and 8 – 'Lost in the Jungle', 'Evening' or 'On the Dodgems'. These pieces may be played as solos or with the piano accompaniments. Alternatively, you may choose any piece from *Party Time!* for Cello (published by ABRSM Publishing). If you select a piece from *Party Time!* or decide to play one of the pieces in this book with its accompaniment, either your accompanist or the examiner will play it with you. Your teacher will help you to choose the right piece.

Lost in the Jungle

Timothy Hewitt-Jones

Evening

With gentle movement ♩ = c.77

Timothy Hewitt-Jones

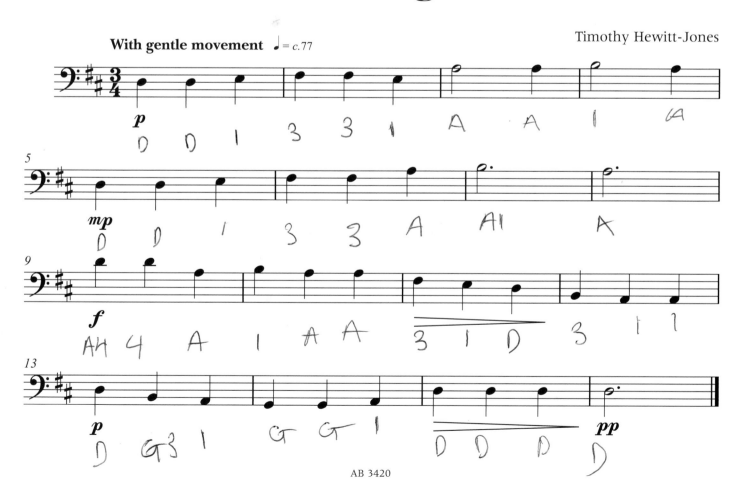

On the Dodgems

3 Own Choice Piece

We would like you to play this with either your accompanist or the examiner, so you need to choose a piece with a piano accompaniment. As we want you to play something you really enjoy, we have left the choice up to you. If you like, you can play one of the set pieces from this book with its accompaniment, as long as it is different from you first piece! Whichever piece you choose, remember to bring the piano part for whoever is accompanying you.

4 Listening Games

In these games the examiner will be playing pieces of music like the examples printed below.

Game A: Clapping the beat

In this first game, the examiner will play a short piece in 2 or 3 time. You should join in as soon as possible by clapping or tapping the beat.

All music has a beat, so you can practise this game at home with your friends whenever you are listening to music on the radio or a recording.

Anon. (adapted)

Purcell

Game B: Echoes

In this game, the examiner will clap two simple two-bar rhythms in 2 or 3 time. After each one, you should clap the rhythm back to the examiner in time and as an echo. The examiner will count in two bars before the first rhythm.

Practise this game at home with a friend or parent. Did you clap *exactly* the same rhythm? Did you clap it back in rhythm or was there a pause?

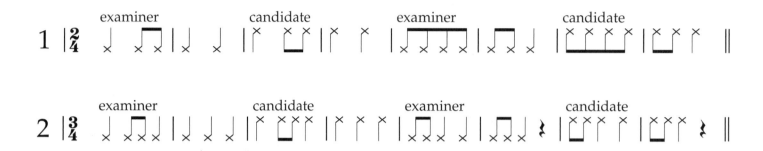

Game C: Finding the notes

Now the examiner will play a group of three notes to you, two times through. The game is to sing these notes back to the examiner after the second playing. They will be played in 'free time', so you don't need to worry about the rhythm. If you don't want to sing, you can play the notes on the G string of your cello, in which case the examiner will play a group using only G, A and B – you have to find all three notes, including the starting note! Here are some examples:

Game D: What can you hear?

In this last game, listen as the examiner plays another short piece of music. The examiner will want to know whether the piece was played loudly or quietly (the 'dynamic' of the piece), or whether it was fast or slow (the 'tempo' of the piece). The examiner will choose one of these and tell you which one to listen out for before he or she plays.

Practise this game at home with your friends whenever you are playing or listening to a piece of music.

i) Is this piece loud or quiet?

ii) Is this piece fast or slow?

Fun Page

Music is written down on five lines known as a 'stave'. A few empty staves are printed below: you can use these to practise drawing notes, rests, clefs and time signatures (if you don't understand any of these words, ask your teacher or look in *First Steps in Music Theory*, published by ABRSM). Or you can write down some tunes of your own.

Word Search

This word search contains 12 musical words, listed below. How many can you find? Do you know what they all mean?

A	S	F	P	D	J	U	C	S	E
S	L	P	I	T	C	H	E	T	I
T	U	R	Z	F	P	T	L	R	H
A	R	M	Z	Q	E	K	L	I	T
V	I	W	I	A	R	C	O	N	E
E	G	C	C	J	D	B	N	G	M
D	Y	N	A	M	I	C	D	Z	P
P	A	Y	T	X	S	I	F	A	O
I	B	K	O	H	R	G	M	C	U
C	L	E	F	B	O	W	I	N	G

Words to find:
stave
bowing
pitch
arco
cello
pizzicato
string
bridge
tempo
clef
slur
dynamic

We hope you enjoyed doing the Prep Test and look forward to seeing you at Grade 1!

02/15   Printed in England by Halstan & Co. Ltd, Amersham, Bucks